I0149339

Devotions of A Saint

A Short Book of Psalms & Poetry

Dr. Paula Price

FLAMING VISION PUBLICATIONS

©2019 in the United States of America

Unless otherwise indicated, all scriptural quotations are from the King James Version of the Bible.

Devotions of a Saint: A Short Book of Psalms & Poetry

Published by Flaming Vision Publications

Tulsa, Oklahoma 74136

ISBN 1-886288-18-6

Foreword

This collection of poems and psalms are the fruit of many hours of prayer and devotion. In many ways, they voice the arduous journey a new comer must travel to learn the Lord. Beginning with shock and awe the path to acceptance and settlement has high highs and low lows. Those new to Jesus Christ know and resolve bit by bit all that He to comprehend what makes Him their Savior and Lord. Throughout the journey, the pathways to meeting and living at peace with Him well show themselves slowly and on occasion, painfully. These writings resonate the major processes well, poeticizing and psalmodizing the trials and tests, and victories over novice temptations that only the Lord can bring one through.

The Lord Jesus exhorts us to love the Lord our God with all of our being and all we possess. Upon being saved by Him, I found falling in love with Him easy and at times raw. Learning Jesus Christ was exhilarating, living with Him was not always the case. You see loving our Father with our dark and frail human love is spontaneous. After all, Romans 5 tells us He shed His love abroad in our hearts. In the beginning our human love for Christ surfaces under our control where we dictate it. Loving God with His love is harder and often unsettling because neither He nor His ways are like us. Our affections were nurtured under the rules of the flesh. God's love is nowhere near ours and as I learned Him, I realized how fragile though genuine my affections were compared to His. As I became acquainted with the God, I truly fell in love with Him. Still, despite my sincerity and best attempts to equal His I discovered many times how flawed my human capacity for His kind of love is.

Getting acquainted with our God, our Father, our Savior, and our King is not always a smooth process for us. It often involves skirting agonizing emotional mountain and struggling through bitter terrains. I found my journeys through deep, deep heart and soul valleys to enter His truth and have it enter and consume me. Regularly, I would leave His presence wondering if I would make or if He even wanted me to. Of course, those moments were ludicrous but that is how stunned I was at what learning and knowing a God I mentioned and thought of for decades really took.

Exhilarating moments quickly fled as His sovereignty met my humanity. Often, I awoke with splendorous dreams that sobered me with equally staggering costs. Prayer times were consoling and often scolding in the beginning as I pressed into God beckoning me to come up higher. Something He calls us to during our pilgrimage here on earth. At every step and turn Our heavenly Father perfected me to desire and endure more and more of His magnificence; to satisfy both our longing for His glories to be revealed in me. The price of the ecstasies I enjoy in His presence didn't come cheap nor where they swift. Every delight was tempered with the wisdom of knowing that to be with the Almighty, yea to become one with Him demands all we hide, hold dear, and hope He'll accept on our terms. "Devotions of a Saint" expresses why we must abandon all to get a small glimpse of our Father's glory divine.

Devotions of a Saint reflects the spirit of our glorious calling, which is not only to be sojourners here on earth, but also to overcome life's battles and inherit Jesus Christ's promises as we confront and conquer our own weaknesses. I pray this book provides you with the comforts and insight I relished during periods of testing and refinement; something no serious saint of God can avoid.

Author of
Devotions of a Saint

Contents

The Invitation

*"Come to Me, all you who labor and are heavy laden,
and I will give you rest. Take My yoke upon you and learn
from Me, for I am gentle and lowly in heart, and you will find rest
for your souls. For My yoke is easy and My burden is light."
"On the last day, that great day of the feast, Jesus stood
and cried out, saying, 'If anyone thirsts, let him come
to Me and drink. He who believes in Me, as the Scripture
has said, out of his heart will flow rivers of living water.'"
Matthew 11:28-30 and John 7:37-38 NKJV*

Adorations and affections for the Lord of all creation. All
You nations of the earth come worship Him.

Magnify the Lamb of God, Who was slain to erase
human sin.
Bow down and present your offering.

Bring your gift of first fruits to the Master Who has
mercy on
You. And enter His inner courts by His Spirit and His
truth.

Give the Lord Who, Almighty God the praises due only
to Him.
Sanctify yourselves by His holiness now dwelling
within.

Rejoice in fellowship and communion with the Creator
Of all time. Feast at the banquet table of the One Who
gives
Sight to the blind.

Consume to the full that manna from above.
Soar to new heights in faith and strength
On the wings of heaven's Holy Dove.

Let sweet praise usher you into His Presence,
Washed in His blood. Overflowing with His love,
Come all Creation; worship every worlds'
marvelousness.

Receive His invitation to approach His immaculate light,
Take this opportunity to rest from earth's wearisome
fights.
Change your soul's garments, put on His robe of
righteousness,

Accept His offer to heal you and saturate you with His
hallowed, holy bliss.

Jesus says: "Come, ye blessed of my Father, inherit the kingdom prepared for you from the foundation of the world." Matthew 25:34

The Secrets Of His Heart

*"That the God of our Lord Jesus Christ, the Father of glory,
May give unto you the spirit of wisdom and revelation in the
Knowledge of him: The eyes of your understanding being
Enlightened; that ye may know what is the hope of his
Calling, and what the riches of the glory of his Inheritance
in the saints." "Now to him that is of Power to stablish you
according to my gospel, And the preaching of Jesus Christ,
According to the revelation of the mystery, Which was kept
secret since the world began…"*
Ephesians 1:17-18, Romans 16:25

He spoke with me again this afternoon, telling me the
things
He wanted me to do. Sharing His needs openly with me,
Consuming me by His wisdom and mysteries.

Each time we commune is more memorable than the
time before. As my Savior from His blessed heart, His
secrets to me outpour.

A miracle that boggles my mind is that He confides in
me.
What the rest of this world still hold as a mystery.

Opening His own soul to fill mine with His private,
deeper truths. Revelation after revelation
Make me fit for the Savior's use.

Oh Holy One, Jehovah My God, my being overflows
With endless Hallelujahs! I'll forever cherish and
Protect the priceless wisdom I receive.
Faithfully using it to help others to desire Him and
believe.

Eternal Flames

"And in the midst of the seven candlesticks one like
Unto the Son of man, clothed with a garment down
To the foot, and girt about the paps with a
Golden girdle. His head and his hairs were
White like wool, as white as snow; and
His eyes were as a flame of fire; And his feet
Like unto fine brass, as if they burned in a furnace;
And his voice as the sound of many waters."
"But upon mount Zion shall be deliverance.
And there shall be holiness; and the house of Jacob
Shall possess their possessions. And the house of Jacob
Shall be fire, and the house of Joseph a flame,
And the house of Esau for stubble, and they shall
Kindle in them, and devour them; and there shall
Not be any remaining of the house of Esau;
For the LORD hath spoken it."
Revelation 1:13-15 and Obadiah 1:17-18 KJV

Eternal flames burn within me.
Lord, they burn for You.

Eternal fires roar and rage within me.
Lord, for the excellence of You.

Eternal life removes my darkness.

Eternal power drowns my fears.
Whispers of love, acceptance, and affection,
Forever echo in my ears.

A soul once sunk deep in sin. A heart once
Warped by ugliness within.

Now radiate with salvation's glorious light.
Totally free from corruption and blight.

Before, bound and doomed to die.
No one to care for me or listen to my cries.

Now consumed by this heavenly fire –
Loosed to serve the God worthy of all desire;
Engulfed in heaven's altar fire.

Eternal flames burn within me.
Lord, they burn for You.
Eternal fires roar and rage within me, as
They burn for the excellence of You.

Hallowed Be Christ The Lamb

*"The next day John saw Jesus coming toward him,
And said, "Behold the Lamb of God who takes away
The sin of the world!"
John 1:29 NKJV*

Christ the Lamb of God –
My portion and my feast.

The Holy Bread of Heaven;
My Soul's delightful treat.

The precious blood that flowed from
Calvary fills my blessing cup.

A wondrous glow that warms me
Every time I feel His touch.

How my soul thrives on Your goodness,
My life daily enriched by Your food.

15

My every hunger fulfilled, desire met,
Whenever Your Spirit within me moves.

Better than the delicacies of my world,
You satisfy my every appetite.

Brighter than the greatest flame,
You break through my darkest night.

Christ, the centerpiece of Paradise,
Salvation – Eden's most precious prize.

As I come to Your sinless world sublime
I rejoice to know, when I do,
I anticipate the day when we live as one for all time.

Always expressing my deepest gratitude
For you becoming mine.

Jesus King of kings you are
And will always be my greatest find.

Hallelujah Lord, I do love you so.

Manna Of Life

"I am the bread of life. He who comes to Me shall never
Hunger, and he who believes in Me shall never thirst.
This is the bread which comes down from heaven,
That one may eat of it and not die. I am the living bread
Which came down from heaven. If anyone eats of this
Bread, he will live forever; and the bread that I shall
Give is My flesh, which I shall give for the life of the world."
John 6:35, 50-51 NKJV

The Godhead's manna of life embodied itself in a Man;
Who was sent from heaven to reveal to us God's plan.

Faithful and dutiful to God's this world's mysterious life;
Entrusted to His only begotten son, Jesus Christ.

Our Lord opened blind eyes and healed ravaged souls;
Unstopped deaf ears with the gospel He told.

Christ searched and sought to gather the children of
Abraham; with whom He made his first covenant,
saying

Jehovah, I Am.
He fed those who were starving for more
Than natural food; giving them the only meal that
Would do them any good.

And when His message of the Kingdom had been fully
Preached. God the Son was sentenced to die so all
Nations might be reached.

In His life He labored gathering Israel, Jacob's seed.
Knowing that only by dying could He meet
All humanity's needs.

Through the cross He delivered all mankind from the
grave.
By rising from the dead, even Gentiles would be saved.

Before ascending into the heavens He told His followers,
"Feed My sheep", and I will give them My Father's life,
And it shall never cease.

Ascending on high, never more to die. Our Savior,
Jesus still feeds us His manna of Life.

Mixed with His blood and powered by His Spirit,
Heaven's manna, called angel's food,
Keeps us forever near and dear to Him.

He Has Given Unto Us

"How excellent is they lovingkindness O God!
Therefore the children of men put their trust
Under the shadow of thy wings. They shall
Be abundantly satisfied with the fatness of
Thy house; and thou shalt make them drink of
The river of thy pleasures. For with thee is the
Fountain of life; in thy light they shall see light."
Psalm 36:7-9 KJV

God gives us blessings richly to enjoy. And prepared for
Us an inheritance that shall never be destroyed.

Glimpses of heaven dart across my eyes, as the raptures
Of Christ's glory bubble up inside.

Merely a foretaste of what lies ahead. For those honored
To rise – like him from the corruptions of the dead.

Multitudes of angels fill the sky; poised to welcome
home
The church, the Messiah's Bride.

Mansions without end and wealth untold. Generous
gifts
From the Father bountifully unfold.

What the eye has not seen. What the ear has not heard.
Is
Suddenly laid before us, as God promised in His word.

Days without end. No sun needed to shine. As we
partake
Of the delights and splendors of creation's Grandeur
Divine.

Tarry Here Awhile

"Wait on the Lord: be of good courage, and he shall
Strengthen thine heart; wait, I say, on the Lord. But
They that wait upon the Lord shall renew their strength;
They shall run and not be weary; They shall walk and not faint."
Psalm 27:14 and Isaiah 40:31

"Tarry here with me awhile," said my Savior
Sweetly with that gentle smile.

With eyes warm and shining bright, He
Beckons me to drop all and come aside.

The errands will wait and the work will go
On. But precious moments in Jesus' love
Should not be denied.

The quiet is so still one instinctively
Knows, how to permit the Savior's love to
sweeten the longing soul.

So many treasures beckon those approaching
Heaven's gate. It's a wonder what makes us
So often put God on hold.

Is it only when life's piles have stolen our
Smiles, that we feel the need to tarry with
The Savior for a while?

Why aren't His delightful fellowship and communion
from Christ's refreshing fountain of love enough, to
make us drop
Everything and rush into the arms of the
Redeemer we love and trust?

But when His love is deeply burned within one thing
Is for sure. When He beckons us to
Tarry with Him, we'll come quickly because
We simply can't postpone His love and passion
anymore.

When You've Found Jesus

"To open their eyes, and to turn them from
Darkness to light, and from the power of Satan unto God,
That they may receive forgiveness of sins, and inheritance among
them
Which are sanctified by faith that is in me."
"And the son said unto him, Father, I have sinned against heaven,
And in thy sight, and am no more worthy to be called thy son.
But the father said to his servants, Bring forth the best robe,
And put it on him; and put a ring on his hand, and shoes on his feet:
And bring hither the fatted calf, and kill it; and let us eat, and be
merry:
For this my son was dead, and is alive again; he was lost, and is
found.
And they began to be merry."
"Therefore if any man be in Christ, he is a new creature:
old things have passed away; behold, all things are become new."
Acts 26:18, Luke 15:21-24, and 2 Corinthians 5:17 KJV

When dark shadows turn to day. When once lost,
You find your way. When the still small
Voice speaks in your heart and you know life's
Given you a new start.

When the fog lifts from your head. And the webs of
Life you no longer dread. It can only mean one thing.

You finally received salvation's redeeming King.
When these glories overtake you, you have found Jesus.

When the weights of the world roll off your back. And
You're free from Satan's straps. When you know where
You're going, and where you're at. It means you have
Found the Lord Jesus.

Questions now answered, prayers now heard, a hunger
Gnaws within you for God's holy word. Right is right,
Wrong is clearly wrong. Where you were once weak,
Suddenly you are now strong.

When you finally understand why, and know for
yourself
The Almighty's truth from the world's lies.
Tears of hopelessness now gone, replaced
With uncanny contentment inside; when at last you can
Say I no longer desire to sin and everyday you see a new
way to win.
It is because and only because you have
Found the Lord Jesus.

Welcome to the family of God "of whom the whole
family
In heaven and earth is named." Ephesians 3:15.

Heaven's Work In My Soul

"And the blood of Jesus Christ His Son cleanses us
From all sin. That we may be partakers of His
Holiness." I John 1:7b and Hebrews 12:10b NKJV

He is washing the stained fabric of my fleshly garment.
Laundering and purging my coat from sin.

Cleansing every spot brought to His throne,
Pressing every wrinkle before I can go home.

Though the pressure is great, the trials very
Hard, the afflictions often more than I can take.

I know my Savior, the Lamb of God, shares my
Load, strengthening me for His name's sake.

Side by side, hand in hand, we stand
Together as one.

I commit my soul for Him to have and to hold,
Trusting fully in the Father, His Spirit, and His Son.

The Incense Of Praise

"Then another angel, having a golden censer,
Came and stood at the altar. He was given
Much incense, that he should offer it with the
Prayers of all the saints upon the golden altar
Which was before the throne. And the smoke of
The incense, with the prayers of the saints, ascended
Before God from the angel's hand." "Therefore
By Him let us continually offer the sacrifice of
Praise to God, that is, the fruit of our lips, giving
Thanks to His name."
Revelation 8:3-4 and Hebrews 13:15 NKJV

Songs of adoration and prayers of faith rise up
To meet the King. In loving devotion we turn from
Ourselves to offer sweet sacrifices to the Maker of
everything.

Make your way to the Godhead's holy place to commune
with the Lord of mercy and grace. Separate yourselves
to see Him face to face.

Offer our Savior sacrifices, spiritual gifts that soothe and
Please His heart. For the Lord your God, and His

Slaughtered Lamb yearn for this from those they set
apart.

Fragrances so sweet they fill His sanctuary with
our holy smell. Lingering long after
Our voices are gone, reminding Him of the family
He rescued from hell.

Songs of victory spring forth with saved soul's zeal and
devotion. Ascending to the ears of God revealing our
hearts, and the depths of our grateful emotions.

Christ the King, Hallowed Son of God – release Your
Rivers to flood us with angelic songs of
heartfelt thanks. Continually we offer You the
Highest praise.
HALLELUJAH! HALLELUJAH! HALLELUJAH!

Devotions And Intimacy

"I am the rose of Sharon and the lily of the valleys.
He that dwellth in the secret place of the most High
Shall abide under the shadow of the Almighty."
Song of Solomon 2:1 And Psalm 91:1 KJV

Precious strokes from Christ's pleasant hand gently
Caress my soul. I meditate in my heart on how
God Almighty could want me so.

A soft whisper filled with life tells me what I mean
To Him – why I was worth the price of His blood to
Buy me back from sin.

My mind listens to every word, I marvel at His pure
Love. As I drift on His holiness, I thank my Savior
Whom I call my Sovereign beloved.

My heart melts anew at His tender touch. So familiar
And yet so delicious, I silently think to myself, "I really
Need these moments so much."

Excitement, contentment, and ardent affection fill

Every second of our intimacy. Rolling away every
Load, my savior truly takes care of me.

Awakenings of pleasure never known before, make
Every visit to His throne
A respite this world could never conceive, each time my
Savior and I are alone.

Our Faithful High Priest

"So also Christ glorified not himself to be made an
High priest; but he that said unto him, THOU ART
MY SON, TO DAY HAVE I BEGOTTEN THEE. As He
Saith also in another place, THOU ART A PRIEST
FOREVER AFTER THE ORDER OF MELCHISEDEC."
Hebrews 5:5,6 KJV

Not too often do I think about Your continual
Intercession for me. Not often enough do I even
consider
Your present-day ministry.

Far too many times, I've treated Your perpetual
Work much too casually. Even feeling on occasion
Until I die there is little for You to do for me.

And then something happens, I box myself in.
In a moment I find I allowed my soul to fall back into
Secret sin.

Then I realize I needed a way out; a way to
Restore myself to you to remove sin's burdensome

Fears, and doubts.

Again I painfully recall that due to humanity's fall, I am
Helpless outside of Your place. And if it weren't for Your
High Priestly ministry I would remain separated
From You; pathetically severed from your redeeming
grace.

Swiftly, during these times You remind as my
Comforter and Advocate that my Great High Priest,
Jesus the Messiah ever lives to intercede for me.

Immediately I go to where I've come to know
Forgiveness; and the healing balm that shall never
cease.
Where the burden of my sin and its weakness are
purged
To restore my soul with Your calm and Your peace.

As I trust the prayers of my Savior, for the virtue that
Ever keeps my soul. I surrender my will to God's
mercies,
And I yield to His Spirit's control.

Once again restored, as though I'd never sinned before,
I come boldly to the Father's tent. With arms
outstretched

He gladly welcomes me, to dwell once again,
Righteously in His presence.

For my Great High Priest, my Faithful Intercessor, once
more triumphantly pleaded my case. And forgiveness by
His blood brought me back to where I was before,
confidently walking potently in God's grace.

Jesus, thank You for eternally ministering at the altar of
my
Heart. Thank You for consecrating me wholly, for
sealing me
And devotedly setting me apart.

Oh Great Shepherd, Captain of my soul, Anchor of my
faith.
Your gifts are more precious than earthly riches, You
alone
Pass me through heaven's gate.

How good it is to know, because You loved me before
the world was, You slaughtered Yourself to intercede
perpetually for my Soul's purity and growth.

Even now when I think I can handle my life, and take
good
Enough care of me. You remind me that it was Your

Sacrifice that paid the awful price to loose me from
captivity.

Far better than the high priests of old, who daily
ministered
In tabernacles of wood, stone and gold. You Lord once
for all
Offered the perfect gift. And today by Your power I will
Always live because of what You were not too selfish to
give.

Even now, it's hard for me to understand; why You
would Make my heart your sanctuary, ever living to
minister in
This tabernacle not made by human hands.

Die In The Faith

"And these all, having obtained a good report through Faith,
Received not the promise: God having provided Some better thing
For us, that they without us should Not be made perfect."
"And the smoke of their torment Ascendeth up forever and ever:
and They have no rest day or Night who worship the beast And his
image, And whosoever receiveth the mark of his name. Here is the
patience of The saints: here are they that keep The
commandments of God, and the Faith of Jesus. And I Heard a voice
from heaven saying unto me, Write, Blessed Are the dead which
die in the Lord from henceforth: Yea,
Saith the Spirit, that they may rest from their labours; and Their
works Do follow them."
Hebrews 11:39,40 and Revelation 14:11-13 KJV

To those who loved Him to the point of losing
Their heads, hear what the Spirit says to those
Faithful and true to His righteousness.

Hear the Spirit celebrate all who didn't yield to
darkness and refused the Satan's best. Join in
heaven's delight over the saints preferring to die a
martyr's death.

35

Lift up the cup of victory filled with the Lamb's wine
of blessedness. They confessed Jesus Christ as
Savior and Lord, declaring His sovereignty with
their last breath.

Creation exalts these martyred souls' testimony;
they passed their earthly tests.
With the dignity and supremacy as children of I Am.
The Godhead rewards Christ's Bride with the
wedding
Supper of the Lamb.

Jesus Christ the Faithful Witness with heaven's
elders, living creatures, and angels without number,
lead believers worthy of the treasures laid up by the
Lord,

.

Extending His scepter to His faithful ones in
The world, to His adored He says,
"For you the battle is over, earth's kingdoms are
Now the Lord's and yours"

The Sovereign says, your sin is purged, your robes
are Made white by the lives you gladly sacrificed.
"Come you blessed of My Father, dwell forever in
His opulent light."

In life, His purified saints adored Him, heeding all
He had to say. Now the darkness is behind them, as
They rejoice in the Lord's never-ending Day.
The table now set; the hall filled with Jesus'
justified; the long-awaited words ring out;
"Come, my faithful ones to the wedding prepared
for
My bride. Spend eternity in my temple standing
always
by My side."

"And the Spirit and the bride say, Come." Revelation
22:17.

ENTER YOU HOLY ONES, INTO THE GLORIOUS JOY OF YOUR LORD!

Going Home

"Giving thanks to the Father who has qualified us to be partakers
of the inheritance of the saints in the light. He has delivered us
from the power of darkness and conveyed us into the kingdom
of the Son of His love, in whom we have redemption through His
blood, the forgiveness of sins." "Most assuredly, I say to you, he
who hears My word and believes in Him who sent Me has
everlasting life, and shall not come into judgment, but has
passed from death into life."
Colossians 1:12-13 and John 5:24 NKJV

I'm leaving hell with its terrors and death.
For I heard my Savior say,
"This your day to ascend from sin's fiery prison and
debt."

Long enough I have wallowed in the murky
Waters of Mortality.

Heeding spiteful voices every day, yielding to soul
Sicknesses and vile hostilities.

Fighting to be free from the throes of horror and
agony.
Knowing that certainly a God of love and power
Must have something better for me.

Ready to live free, I made up my mind to latch
On to hope, and flee hell's futility and grime,
I must take a stand, free me from
what my soul can no longer endure.
I simply cannot let myself stay bound,
Continue living a dead life; that's for sure.

I must choose right and forsake all wrong, if I am to
once And for all leave doom's pit. Decision made, heart
resolved, I hear a still small voice call my name.
It tells me to obey, do what He says, and by His side I
will eternally sit.

God's voice told me to just turn right and follow
The way His suffering paved.
Take the first step, stay on the godly path,
And soon I'd know I was saved.

No, don't look back. Don't turn my head. Don't

Even consider what's now dead.
Fix my mind on the Lamb's cleansing flow,
Focus on the wounds Jesus Christ took in my stead.

If I hesitate one bit, I might forfeit
God's most precious gift,
Fall backward and stumble once again into hell's pit.

I hear Him calling me, my heart follows His words –
Oh what a beautiful sound.
Arising ever so slowly, I'm getting closer to it,
ascending
From hell, I'm no longer lost, I am found.

There I made it, the shackles are loosed, the noose is
gone,
Finally free from hell's dark gloom.

There He is the Savior, Whose voice called me out,
Of the hopeless mire of Satan's doom.

So Shall We Ever Be With The Lord

"Then the King will say to those on His right hand,
'Come, you blessed of My Father, inherit the kingdom
Prepared for you from the foundation of the world.' And
There shall be no more curse, but the throne of God and
Of the Lamb shall be in it and His servants shall serve Him.
They shall see His face, and His name shall be on their
Foreheads."
Matthew 25:34 and Revelation 22:3-4 NKJV

Listen, listen! Lend God your ear. The time of
Your rapture Has drawn near.

You can hear the heavens praising, singing aloud
Holy, holy, holy! Father, Son, and Holy Ghost.

The sky falls away, not a cloud to be seen
In its place heaven's families have gathered to

Welcome God's church, a massive host.

For the day of His salvation has come. Parting
Clouds in the sky for the coming of God the Son, He is
almost here!

For some it is midnight, for others it's the noonday
sun, It won't be long before Judah's Lion shows up.
In an instant the Messiah is in sight, the catching
Away is here.

Suddenly! We're in the air, passing quickly through
The fading clouds. Just as He said He would, He came.
I can Hear the mighty trumpets sound.
His word grafted in our souls, His holy seal in our
foreheads, as we pass through the gate, we are
inscribed with His Almighty Name.

Oh how glorious the splendors of our Lord upon His
throne. God's new creation unite with His holy angels
The Redeemer's church finally comes home.

God's words ring out clearly above the shouts of
praise,
To His ecclesial Bride, He says. "I've waited a long
time for my church sing my salvation song this way."

"At last I've done it! I've wrought My mightiest work. I caught away My Bride. At last I've raptured My church."

"Sing out you holy ones, who know My power and My Mercy and My Grace. From henceforth and forever, Even when time is no more. You'll relate to your Heavenly Father face to face."

Cleanse Oh Healing Flow

*"But he was wounded for our transgressions, he was
Bruised for our iniquities: the chastisement of our
Peace was upon him: and with his stripes we are healed."
Isaiah 53:5 KJV*

Heal the body oh Head of the flock. Cleanse Your
church
With the flow that never stops.

Open up blind eyes, unstop deaf ears. Wipe away,
Dear
Lord, every hurt and tear.

Bind up the brokenhearted. Heal the souls life has
Bruised. Tenderly console and renew the battered
And abused.

Flow oh flow, that precious priceless stream. Pour
Out from Your living rivers, tarnished souls to clean.

Oh cleansing flow wash us, cleanse us, heal us and fill
us, We are the vessels God Almighty has sealed.

Make us sparkling beams of light in this world,
Your Spirit indwelling us, leading through the
darkness,
Preserving our souls from hell.

Equip us by Your word to carry out Your plan. To
Bring the saving grace of Jesus Christ to every
human.

Then move us to Your holy mountain filled with Your
hallowed might.
Sanctify us holy by your word of truth, that we as
your army may win this worldly fight.
Scrub away every blemish, smooth out what flesh has
marred, breathe on us Faithful Creator
The love that remove our soul's scars.

Fit us to partake of heaven's hallowedness.
And when our work in earth is through.
Swiftly bring us Dear Lord home to Your eternal rest.

Peering Into
The Savior's Eyes

*"And I saw heaven opened, and behold a white horse; and he that
sat upon him was called Faithful and True, and righteousness he
doth judge and make war. His eyes were as a flame of fire, and on
his head were many crowns; and he had a name written, that no
man knew, but he himself. And he was clothed with a vesture
dipped in blood: and his name is called The Word of God." "Thou
wilt shew me the path of life: in thy presence is fulness of joy; at
thy right hand there are pleasures for evermore."
Revelation 19:11-13 and Psalm 16:11 KJV*

I look into eyes bright with fire, peering from
The soul of God's altar flame.

I still marvel at the joy I felt, on the day my
Savior to me freed me from sorrow and pain.

Amazed at His purity. No spot,
No blemish, no sin, no shame.

Only the luminant light of the world,
The God-Man who died and rose again.

Stunningly beautiful, startling bright. How lovely are
Those eyes that probe my soul; erasing its sadness
He Turns its gloom into His purest gold.

One glance from His eyes and my old self died,
Suddenly I'm at His side.

Powerfully drawn to the light in my Savior's eyes
I walk into the God's Garden of Paradise.

Visions Of The Holy Land

"I knew a man in Christ above fourteen years ago, (whether
In the body, I cannot tell; or whether out of the body, I cannot tell:
God knoweth) such an one caught up to the third heaven.
And I knew such a man, (whether in the body or out of the
Body, I cannot tell: God knoweth;) How that he was caught
Up into paradise, and heard unspeakable words, which it is not
Lawful for a man to utter."
II Corinthians 12:2-4 KJV

Visions of beauty give me peeks into eternity.
Overwhelming excellence swallow whenever
I enter the world God shares with me.

Purer than eyes can stand. Sweeter
Than every delight no one can understand.
The true holy
Land, the one not made by mortal hands.

Stateliness waits beyond the clouds for God faithful
Humble ones.

Rays brighter than a sunburst penetrate their heart
because His Spirit and blood make them His children.

Colors more brilliant than all His rainbows.
Only Illustrious majesty abides on High, ruling in
righteousness with dignity greater than the fallen can
know.

Radiance overflows into every corner of God's true
holy land. Disclosing itself to those destined to reign
there, Impressing upon them what He holds in store
for all who live by His commands.

Holy Spirit opens to us what we could never before
Christ understand. Stunning to once blinded sight is
the deathless country that Needs no light.

Prepared by our Father, the true and living God, is a
land of opulence and affluence for those who
conquer evil's Fight; If we manage to finish His race,
we get to join Happy shouts of joyful praise with
countless meek souls Already basking in His grace.

Heaven eagerly readies itself for our arrival to the
Most Holy's everlasting Zion; Matchless splendor
No human can imitate clothe us with the garments of
the invisible world of our Father's Messiah.

Picture, if you can, the glorious ages of life before all
time;

Let your mind break its seal on what no earthly being
can divine. Imagine walking, working,
Living in the Creator's first handiwork.
The promised residential reign of God's triumphant
Church,

Imagine if you will, the Most High God's awesome
yearning for you,
Patiently waiting for the day earth receives its due.

See yourself being swept away by His beauty.
Changed in a
Twinkling of an eye you take on His image.

Doors swing open wide and amazingly we all are
ushered
Inside the kingdom that has ruled all ages.

In the land, made by the Son of God's
Holy, powerful hands; God the Son our Creator,
Maker, Sovereign, and Savior stands at the door,
Defying all human phenomenon. But wait there's
More.
Jesus the Messiah is not only heir of God's eternal
holy land, but wonder of wonders, He's also its
Founder,
Which is why He reigns with the Father

Of creation as Monarch and Possessor and creation's
incarnate I Am.

His Majesty Is Waiting

"No man can come to me, except the Father which
hath sent me draw him: and I will raise him up at the last day."
"Behold, I will send my messenger, and he shall prepare
the way before me: and the Lord, whom ye seek,
shall suddenly come to his temple, even the messenger
of the covenant, whom ye delight in: behold, he shall come,
saith the Lord of hosts. But who may abide the day of his coming?
and who shall stand when he appeareth? for he is like a refiner's fire,
and like fullers' soap: And he shall sit as a refiner and purifier of
silver:
and he shall purify the sons of Levi, and purge them as gold and
silver,
that they may offer unto the Lord an offering in righteousness."
"O come, let us worship and bow down: let us kneel before
the Lord our maker. For he is our God; and we are the people of his
pasture,
and the sheep of his hand. Today if ye will hear his voice,
Harden not your heart, as in the provocation,
and as in the day of temptation in the wilderness:"
John 6:44, Malachi 3:1-3, and
Psalm 95:6-8 KJV

Hail! All you throbbing with godly hope,
listen to the call of the King.

Enter the inner Chambers,
To wine and dine with His Majesty
Hurry! He's waiting.

Approach, come closer, nearer
Than you've ever been before.
Creation's Majesty is summoning you
To visit with Him behind the door.

Drop your burdens, leave your
Sin, walk away from oppression, strife
And despair. Turn away,
Forsake the treasures of the
Dead. God is inviting for you
To come. To feast with the Prince of Life.
Hurry! The Lord is waiting.

Give up your wanderings and turn
From this life's floundering. Step up, take
Your place beside the Son's throne.
Yours is a special call that is not for all, you're chosen
because you made Him your very own.
Don't delay! Reverence this day, because
The Maker is waiting.

Now is your time, today is your day to live a new
way.

Hark! Do you hear that still small voice?
Today, if you Will hear, harden not your heart.
Let down your guard, make eternity's Majesty your
choice. Will you follow Jesus or will you not?

Choose ye this day whom you will
Serve. Pick right now who will be
Your fear. The Spirit is waiting,
Listening for your words. Which
Voice will you let your heart hear?

Let go of your busy work. Lay down
Those aimless desires. Place your will
In the Master's plan, surrender to God's
Purifying fire, forego your human desires,
Make your wants those of the Son of Man.

Hurry, oh please hurry, creation's Majesty is waiting!

The Wait

"As the hart panteth after the water brooks,
So panteth my soul after thee, O God. My soul
Thirsteth for God, for the living God: when
Shall I come and appear before God?"
Psalm 42:1-2 KJV

Jesus, I love You in ways too deep to express.
And daily when we are together, I drink thirstily
from
Your graciousness.

How many times have I cried out to You
In the fullness of Your joy. Asking when
Time will come when I won't have
To leave You anymore.

How pale things of this life become, in the light of
Your preciousness. How feeble its treasures
compared to your Heavenly treasures and rest.

Longing fills my being as I continually reach
For You, hoping every morning I'll awake

To find I'm forever with You.

Oh, how I long to be with You Jesus.
I've had enough of the earth and its dirt;
I cherish the times we share, although
When we part it always hurts.

But I know Your ways are perfect and often
Past finding out. Still I won't be fully content
'Til I'm abiding in Your incorruptible house.

Oh, how I long to be with you Jesus, and to
Relish loving You. I think ceaselessly about lavishing
You With all my praise. I need to be with so much, it
is hard to Get through some of my days.
For you I hold endless thank offerings in my spirit
and soul that I plan to lay at your feet.
They're my thanksgiving for your bountiful blessings
untold.

Get me ready for you by humbling my soul.
Take over my will bring my life under your Holy
Spirit's control.
Fill my being, get me ready to leave this world when
You Return to judge and replace this earth after it
burns.

Shekinah's Splendor

*"And the Word was made flesh, and dwelt among us,
(and we beheld his glory, the glory as of the only
Begotten of the Father,) full of grace and truth."*
John 1:1 KJV

Shekinah is the word given to Your glory.
Omnipotent describes Your mighty power.

Brilliant declares Your light, and eternal
Alone teaches us Your immortal life.

Holy is the one word that explains You,
Who lives forever as the Self-Existent One.

We celebrate the Lord God of all worlds, because
He saves us by His first begotten Son.

Scripture named His Jesus, God Emmanuel who came
as a man to die on Calvary's cross. He said He did it to
seek And save Adam lost.
On Calvary we slaughtered the Godhead's Majesty.
Yes, we hung God the Son on an accursed tree.

Sold to die, whipped for the sinner's
Lie, suffering to set many damned souls free.

Once dead, Christ rose as He said, as heaven's eternal
King. Forgiveness in His heart, healing in His hands;
The Father's righteousness in His wings.

How marvelous is the God of all ages!
Who sent His son to die on that wretched
Cross. How faithful is the Son of heaven's
Pages! To leave glory to be crucified to
For the unworthy lost.

But now He lives apart from sin – Shekinah glorified
Destined to die no more. Reigning in eternity's
dazzling Luxury enriching the souls He purchased
and will forever Adore.

God Remained God Though He Became Man

*"Come near to Me, hear this: I have not
Spoken in secret from the beginning;
From the time that it was, I was there. And
Now the Lord God and His Spirit have sent Me."
"But to the Son He says: Your throne, O God, is
Forever and ever; A scepter of righteousness
Is the scepter of Your kingdom. You have
Loved righteousness and hated lawlessness;
Therefore God, Your God, has anointed You with the
Oil of gladness more than Your companions."
Isaiah 48:16 and Hebrews 1:8-9 NKJV*

****

What a wonderful and faithful heart of steadfast
Love in which we trust. Oh so meek and kind are
The hands that mend and keep us.

What a mighty Man we shall all one day behold.
Warrior of all ages, Savior and Friend;
Worth more than the riches our world can ever hold.

What a miracle it is for us to know that God,
Our Creator, filled the body of a man. That He
Should walk in this doomed planet; with the
People He made with His own hands.

That God put His holy deity into the tent of fallen
Flesh; is the eternal riddle that shall forever
Stumble and stymie the faithless.

Scholarly intellects cannot, will never decode His
Secret kept hidden from before all time. Why Creator
God
Would take the form of a human is baffling to every
Dark mind.

Yet for the child of faith there is no mystery.
The God of heaven just wanted a
Family.
He mirrored on earth what heaven begot in its world.
God the Father sent His firstborn to beget humans
Because they too had a destiny.

Who could ever fathom a love so deep? Earthly
Wisdom could never have thought; The Creator
Came as creature. God in flesh became our teacher,
Humbling Himself lower than the souls He sought.

But that is not the end of the mystery. Really, it's just
The beginning. Walking His earth, doing His Father's
Work, dying the death, Jesus Christ rose again
Doing it all without ever sinning.

That amazement today continues to frustrate human
Heads. Could anyone in the form of wicked flesh live
on Earth and die truly sinless?

The debate goes on. It has for thousands of years.
Answering only those with an ear to hear. Yes God,
Did come; in the Person of His Son. Reconciled us to
His
Father, and returned to heaven as the Glorified One.

How exalted is the Sovereign of all the earth that we
bless. For He alone stood faithful to His Father's
Righteousness. How worthy of the songs of praise
To Him we sing. For he submitted His soul to death
To show Himself humanity's originating King.

Unwaveringly He withstood evil's cruelty. Jesus was
Banished to hell. Having never fell He suffered
horribly For humanity's doom; He laid three days
and night bound
In a hand carved clay tomb.

Behind the scenes while His body laid to rest, Jesus
exiled to hell was fighting His Father's cosmic battle
with evil.
He wrested from hell eternity's keys to mortality.
Returning home with the souls Eden lost, the Captain

Of our salvation, today sits enthroned on high as King
of Kings.
Jesus Messiah is the God of every nation because as
its Creator, His death released every human from
death, to reign as His royal new creation.

God A Delight To The Taste

"Oh taste and see that the Lord is good; Blessed is
The man who trusts in Him!"
Psalm 34:8 NKJV

Oh taste and see that the Lord is good. Much sweeter
Than the honey comb.

Come take your bite from the raptures of His life as
You become His beloved, His very own.

Enter the great hall, filled with His love and
Splendor, dine on love Divine.
Your appetites will be satisfied once you drink from
God's life-giving vines.

Clothe yourself in His robes of celebration,

Content yourself with Christ alone as your Savior.
Recline in His peace, let His pleasure be all you seek.
Rejoice always in the Lord's favor.

Shout for joy you glorified ones; let your spirit sing.
Eat 'til
His glory fills you, as you feast on heaven's bread
His manna for the redeemed.
Wallowing in His beauty, swallowed in endless glory
clouds contentedly sit at His feet,
Wearing His yoke, like the ancients, feasting on every
word He spoke, make His wisdom one you keep.

Marriage Covenant

"Marriage is honourable in all, and the bed undefiled:
But whoremongers and adulterers God will judge."
Hebrews 13:4 KJV

"Marriage is a sacred thing," my Lord said me. It is
"An institution I'll honor and treasure
Way beyond infinity."

"When my mind thought to give Adam and his wife
what
Meant most to me. God said marriage came forth as
His
Best sanctuary for human intimacy."

"The love between a man and his wife is a union
Equaled by none. It was meant to show earth's
generations the unity of the Godhead and how it
became One.

Father, Son, and Spirit; so tightly knit together,

Nothing in any world has the power or key piercing
it, Ever."

"And then when I asked Myself, the Lord continued,
what would best commemorate marital love. The
conception
And birth of children is the perfect blessing I
Thought of."

"I sought to show your world the family order we
enjoy
On high. And to give the married something precious
To always remember Me by."

"When man takes his wife and woman yields to his
love, the bond formed between them resembles the
ecstasy we Revel in above."

"Only in the beauty of holiness is such a yoke
crowned.
And in no other enjoinment on earth is God's purist
union Found."

"Companionship and friendship are other reasons I
gave Marriage as a gift to you. In doing so I thought
also to secure your oneness, and to teach you My
most sacred Truths.

Streams of life course through marital intimacy that leave some of each one's soul behind. That is why I ordained marriage to reproduce myself in mankind.

"I further thought to give you before you came to Me. A taste of what life will be for those who imitate my love as it is between We three."

Reserved for you in heaven, is a place of peace, pleasure and prosperity where delights never end. If you are born of my Spirit and transformed to reign with Me, you're Your everlasting life begins.

Held in store for you waits a fear free, debt free, horror free world of genuine liberty. Should you value my salvation and deem my future to be your immortal Destiny.

To let you know that heaven is one, we are all connected here and indivisibly unified. I bestowed what you call marriage upon you to make your conjoined spirits and Souls My bride.

The marriage union is the only way you can grasp with your human minds, what it means to become utterly one and cease to be covenant breakers.

Faithfulness to your marriage vows help you appreciate the everlasting life covenant My Son's shed blood purchased as the first begotten of humanity's Maker.

The Spirit and the Bride say, "Come for all things are now Ready for you to be made new; Enter the joys of your Lord."

About the Author

Paula A. Price is a strong and widely acknowledged international voice on the subject of apostolic and prophetic ministry. She is recognized as a modern-day apostle with a potent prophetic anointing. Active in full-time ministry since 1985, she has founded and established three churches, an apostolic and prophetic Bible institute, a publication company, consulting firm, and global collaborative network linking apostles and prophets together for the purpose of kingdom vision and ventures. Through this international ministry, she has transformed the lives of many through her wisdom and revelation of God's kingdom.

As a former sales and marketing executive, Dr. Price effectively blends ministerial and entrepreneurial applications in her ministry to enrich and empower a diverse audience with the skills and abilities to take kingdoms for the Lord Jesus Christ. A lecturer, teacher, curriculum developer and business trainer, Dr. Price globally consults Christian businesses, churches, schools and assemblies. Over a 30-year period, Dr. Price has developed a superior curriculum to train Christian ministers and professionals, particularly the apostle and the prophet. Her programs often are used in both secular and non-secular environments worldwide.

Although she has written over 25 books, manuals, and other course material on the apostolic and prophetic, she is most recognized for her unique 1,600-term Prophet's Dictionary, and her concise prophetic training manual entitled The Prophet's Handbook. Other releases include The ABC's of Apostleship, a practical guide to the fundamentals of modern apostleship; Divine Order for Spiritual Dominance, a five-fold ministry tool; Eternity's

Generals, an explanation of today's apostle; and When God Goes Silent: Living Life Without God's Voice.

In 2002, Dr. Price created one of the most valuable tools for Christian Ministry called the Standardized Ministry Assessment series. It is a patent pending, destiny discovery tool that tells people who they are in God, what He created them to do, and how He created them to do it. The assessment series pinpoints those called to the church, its pulpit or other ministries, and those who would better serve the Lord outside of the church.

Beside this, Dr. Price has also developed credentialing tools for ministers and professionals, commissioning criteria and practices, along with ceremony proceedings for apostles and prophets. To complement these, she designed extensive educational programs for the entire five-fold officers and their teams.

In addition to her vast experience, Dr. Price has a D.Min. and a Ph.D. in Religious Education from Word of Truth Seminary in Alabama. She is also a wife, mother of three daughters, and the grandmother of two.

Other Titles from Dr. Paula Price

The Prophet's Dictionary: The Ultimate Guide to
Supernatural Wisdom

The Prophet's Handbook: A Guide to Prophecy and Its
Operations

3D: Distress to Success

Before the Garden: God's Eternal Continuum

Money is A Spirit

The Gambler's Faith

Divine Order for Spiritual Dominance

Prophecy: God's Divine Communications Media

Eternity's Generals: The Wisdom of Apostleship

When God Goes Silent

The Five-Fold Ministry Offices

The ABC's of Apostleship Series

www.ingramcontent.com/pod-product-compliance
Lightning Source LLC
LaVergne TN
LVHW051429080426
835508LV00022B/3305